Oh, the Places You'll Eff Up!

A Parody for Your Twenties

JOSH MILLER & PATRICK CASEY
illustrated by GEMMA CORRELL

Ulysses Press
P.O. Box 3440
Berkeley, CA 94703
www.ulyssespress.com

ISBN 978-1-64604-171-8

Printed in the United States
10 9 8 7 6 5 4 3 2 1

Acquisitions Editor: Katherine Furman
Proofreader: Lauren Harrison

Oh,
the Places
You'll Eff Up!

Graduation has come,
and you're feeling no fear.

You've got a college degree!
You'll be rich in a year!

But the world has changed
since your parents were young.
All the jobs have been outsourced
to people far-flung.

Apartments are pricey.
Your relationship is lame.
Suddenly there are twenty-eight
bills in your name.

But are you stressed out?
Your future's in flux!

No, you are not.
You give zero fucks.

Everyone Poops at Work

The job search is going!
Your resume's the best.
But you're under-qualified
for most openings
and too good for the rest.

A year without work causes
your sense of self to unravel.
When asked what you do, you say,
"I took time off to travel."

Your standards have dropped
as you search for a solution.

A janitor?

A bellhop?

Hey, don't forget prostitution!

Then at last you land a job.
Your career is now rolling—
and it only took two years
of Craigslist-ad trolling.

You'll be a "team player,"
work weekends, long hours.
You'll live at your desk—
there's no time for showers!

A promotion is brewing.
The boss says you're a shoo-in!
Then it goes to his nephew,
and your life is in ruin.

You sit in the stall,
playing games on your phone,
or searching for jobs
as you mutter and groan.

You dream of that day
when you finally
can quit.

And walk out the door
telling your boss to
"Eat shit!"

The Very Hungry Roommate

You want your own place? Well come to your senses.
You need a roommate to share your expenses.

Oh, what good friends:
Watching movies!
Playing games!
Drinking so much you can't remember your names.

But his girlfriend won't leave;
he won't help with the dusting.
The sink's full of dishes;
the bathroom's disgusting!

He eats all your food.

He smokes all your weed.

He breaks all your shit.

And in the corner? He peed!

You call a house meeting.
He must clean up his act!
He says he can't make rent,
but he'll pay you right back.

Your friendship has ended;
roommate tensions have caused it.
And thanks to that prick,
you have lost your deposit.

So it's time to strike out
and find a new place,
where you won't have a roommate
all up in your face.

Though the bills break your bank
when you pay them alone,
there's nothing quite like
a home of one's own.

Are You My Girlfriend?

You and your sweetheart try co-habitation.
Hello, home-cooked dinner!
So long, masturbation!

Being together so much
causes the passion to wane.
What was cute in small doses
now drives you insane!

So you ditch the ball and chain,
now you're tied to no one.
The world of adult dating:
Such freedom! Such fun!

Replace your inhibitions
with some one-night affairs.
Gain experience.
Chlamydia!
A pregnancy scare!

His internet profile promised
"well-read, witty, and thin,"
when in fact he's illiterate
and sports more than one chin.

You finally find someone.
Oh, it's a big deal.
You've got a great girl.
This time it's for real.

You think she's **The One**!
Wait. Who's that tagged in her pic?
She *says* you're her boyfriend,
so **who the fuck** is Rick?

After too many a wild night
ends in morning-after rejection,
You pine and you long
for a more lasting connection.

Yes, some nights will be lonely
when you're solo, untethered,
but one day you'll find that person—
and be lonely together.

Where the Wild Things Aren't

Once upon a time you partied epically late.
Now your alarm buzzes at seven, the train leaves at eight.

Work starts at nine, while your brain's in first gear,
and you can't call in sick with "a bad case of beer."

Your suit, shirt, and tie need to be cleaned, starched, and pressed.

No more grabbing from the hamper as a way to get dressed.

Company happy hours can't compare to house parties of yore.
HR doesn't allow **beer pong** or **passing out** on the floor.

When you bedded a dorm mate
and still saw them in class,
the awkwardness was temporary
and well **worth dat ass.**

But coworker sex,
even for an ass you admire,
is a pretty stupid reason
to risk **getting fired.**

Luckily you have something now
that you didn't back then,

a Friday paycheck to bankroll
your party weekend!

The Taking Tree

As you climb up in life,
you'll get bogged down with bills.
For the rent and the phone
and the co-pay for pills.

And just as you achieve
a good financial position,
you'll discover your car
needs a whole new transmission.

Your student loans are immense,
your monthly payments so high.
It'll take years to pay off,
unless you **get lucky and die!**

With all of your bills
amounting to so much,
when out on a date
you'll need to go dutch.

You'll have to put off marriage
till you pull out of this skid.
You can't afford *yourself*,
how could you provide for a kid?

You've effed shit up.
Things are seriously bad.
You're pondering a move...
back in with mom and dad.

Don't worry so much,
money comes and it goes.

You'll keep some, you'll lose some,
like frost-bitten toes.

So whenever life leaves you
tired, angry, or sore,

just be happy you're not
in high school anymore!

About the Contributors

JOSH MILLER and PATRICK CASEY once lived in Minnesota but ran away to Los Angeles. They wrote *The World Reduced to Infographics* and currently write the Fox animated television series *Golan the Insatiable*. Josh is the author of *The Very Hungry Parasite* and *The Zombie's History of the United States*. Patrick once saw a UFO.

GEMMA CORRELL is the author and illustrator of *A Cat's Life*, *A Dog's Life*, *A Pug's Guide to Etiquette*, and *A Pug's Guide to Dating*. Her work has been published by Hallmark, *The New York Times*, and Oxford University Press. She lives in the United Kingdom.

CPSIA information can be obtained
at www.ICGtesting.com
Printed in the USA
LVHW070321040321
680511LV00002B/4

9 781646 041718